Thee Almighty & Insane

CHICAGO GANG BUSINESS CARDS
FROM THE 1970s & 1980s

BY BRANDON JOHNSON

ALMIGHTY & INSANE BOOKS
WWW.ALMIGHTYANDINSANEBOOKS.COM

THIRD EDITION
COPYRIGHT © 2023 BRANDON JOHNSON
ISBN: 978-1-734-58733-3

PRINTED BY AC DOMINIE

SPECIAL THANKS TO EVERYBODY WHO OFFERED STORIES, INFORMATION, AND/OR SUPPORT IN ANY FORM—YOU KNOW WHO YOU ARE.

FOR MORE INFORMATION ON THE HISTORY AND CULTURE OF GANGS IN CHICAGO SEE THE FOLLOWING:

COMPLIMENTS OF CHICAGOHOODZ: CHICAGO STREET GANG ART & CULTURE BY JAMES "JINX" O'CONNOR & DAMEN "MR. C" CORRADO, *THE OLD NEIGHBORHOOD* BY BILL HILLMANN, *SACRED SMOKES* BY THEODORE C. VAN ALST JR., *THEE JERUSALEM GANGSTER* BY EMAD U DEEN, *THE INSANE CHICAGO WAY* BY JOHN M. HAGEDORN, *MY BLOODY LIFE: THE MAKING OF A LATIN KING* BY REYMUNDO SANCHEZ, *ROMANTIC VIOLENCE IN R WORLD* BY MARK WATSON, *LORDS OF LAWNDALE: MY LIFE IN A CHICAGO WHITE STREET GANG* BY MICHAEL SCOTT, *THE ALMIGHTY BLACK P-STONE NATION: THE RISE, FALL, AND RESURGENCE OF AN AMERICAN GANG* BY NATALIE Y. MOORE & LANCE WILLIAMS, *A NATION OF LORDS: THE AUTOBIOGRAPHY OF THE VICE LORDS* BY DAVID DAWLEY, *GANG LEADER FOR A DAY* BY SUDHIR VANKATESH, *UPTOWN* BY BOB REHAK, *BROWN IN THE WINDY CITY: MEXICANS AND PUERTO RICANS IN POSTWAR CHICAGO* BY LILIA FERNANDEZ, *HILLBILLY NATIONALISTS, URBAN RACE REBELS, AND BLACK POWER: COMMUNITY ORGANIZING IN RADICAL TIMES* BY AMY SONNIE & JAMES TRACY, THE FILMS *TRICK BAG* (1974) AND *THE HEART BROKEN IN HALF* (1990), STONEGREASERS.COM, GAYLORDS712.COM, @CHITOWNHOODARTTV, @VINTAGEFIENDS, & CHICAGO'S COLD WAR, TO NAME JUST A FEW.

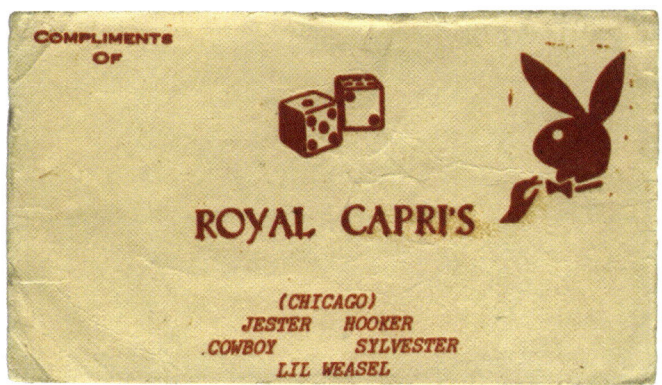

In the attic of our house in suburban Chicago there was a cigar box of my Dad's old belongings: a yellowed copy of Abbie Hoffman's *Steal This Book*, assorted pocket-knives, pelts of thirteen-lined ground squirrels, and other relics of his youth. One object that caught my eye in particular was an aged business card that read "Royal Capri's (Chicago)" in red ink, and listed a series of nicknames: Jester, Hooker, Cowboy, Sylvester, Lil Weasel. It had stock graphics—a pair of dice and *Playboy* bunny logo— and in the top left corner the words "Compliments Of." When I asked about the card, Dad told me his friend made it in their high school's graphic arts class but didn't elaborate further. Being younger at the time, I accepted this answer and left it at that to explore other treasures from the attic.

Later on down the line after moving to New York City, I was back home for a visit and crossed paths with the card again. This time I purloined it for a little independent research and quickly discovered that this card was part of a larger phenomenon native to the Chicagoland area, most prevalent between the 1960s and 1980s, when street gangs made business cards (known colloquially as "compliment cards") displaying their symbols, nicknames, territories, and enemies as a means to assert their pride, recruit new members, and serve as general tokens of affiliation. Less intended, but maybe more significant today is the role of these cards as historical artifacts—not only documenting the specific histories of these gangs and their members, but also the social dynamics of a violent and contentious time period in the city of Chicago.

Many major Chicago street gangs from the 1960s onward found their roots as social athletic clubs, civil rights organizations, and neighborhood greaser gangs. Over time these groups turned at odds with others in their immediate areas, whether due to post-game arguments, culture clash, or physical attempts to reinforce existing social structures. In fact, fighting others soon seemed to be half the point—the other half being a sense of protection and camaraderie. During a time of social and demographic change in Chicago racial tension became a source of conflict, arising as bullying and disputes over territory in tit-for-tat attacks. In the late 1950s and 1960s Puerto Rican and Mexican populations were being pushed out of their Lincoln Park and Near West Side neighborhoods due to a city organized "urban renewal" process and municipal projects including extensions of University of Illinois Chicago and "The Circle" interchange for the Kennedy and Dan Ryan Expressways. These groups ended up in Pilsen on the Lower West Side, Little Village on the Southwest Side, Humboldt Park and West Town on the West Side, and Wicker Park, Bucktown, Logan Square, and other neighborhoods on the North and Northwest Sides. These inter-city migrations, along with a new wave of Latino immigration from Puerto Rico and Mexico in the mid-1960s resulting from civil rights inspired changes by Congress to U.S. immigration policies in the form of the Immigration and Nationality Act of 1965, became a focal point for White and Latino gangs in the 1960s and 1970s. White gangs perceived their role as defending their neighborhoods and way of life from encroaching outsiders as white flight to the suburbs led to more rapid turnover. Latino gangs saw theirs as protecting themselves and their cultures from oppression and racism. Nativism has a long history in the United States, with each wave of newcomers bearing resistance from groups already established. Chicago was no exception, and street-level violence between gangs was in part an expression of this.

But conflict wasn't simply drawn along racial lines. As time went on there was infighting among local gangs of the same races as well as cross-race gang alliances formed from opposition to common enemies. The Folk Nation alliance was organized in 1978 by Larry Hoover, chairman of the Black Gangster Disciples, while imprisoned at Stateville Correctional Center (he's now at federal supermax ADX Florence) in order to control gang activities and protection in the Illinois correctional system. Folk Nation spanned across races, and included gangs such as the Black Gangster Disciples, Two Six, Satan Disciples, Ambrose, Two Two Boys, La Raza, Harrison Gents,

Milwaukee Kings, Ashland Vikings, Orquesta Albany, Spanish Cobras, Latin Eagles, Imperial Gangsters, Latin Disciples, Simon City Royals, North Side Popes, C-Notes, and Paulina Barry Community, among others. A rival alliance, People Nation, was immediately formed in response and included the Vice Lords, El Rukns (a.k.a. Black P. Stones), Mickey Cobras, Four Corner Hustlers, Latin Kings, Insane Unknowns, Spanish Lords, War Lords, Puerto Rican Stones, Insane Deuces, Villa Lobos, Bishops, Latin Counts, Party Players, Gaylords, Jousters, Playboys, Stoned Freaks, and South Side Popes, to name a few. Alliance names and symbols frequently appeared on cards—Folk Nation was represented by pitchforks, hearts with wings, devil's horns/tails, and six-pointed crowns/stars. People Nation symbols were 3-D pyramids, crescent moons, canes, and five-pointed crowns/stars.

Once initiated, these alliances were respected into the 1980s. But after crack hit the streets of Chicago around 1988 the drug trade flourished and serious money was at stake to be made. As organizations became increasingly profit-minded through criminal enterprise the Folk and People alliances continued to exist but could not guarantee peace between members. Chiefs were targeted by law enforcement and imprisoned out of state, causing top down structure through nations to deteriorate and the reality on the streets began to diverge from that in the prisons due to local struggles over drug territory with smaller gangs revolting against subjugation by larger gangs who looked to increase their levels of control and influence. Into the 1990s and beyond members on the street could only remain loyal to those who were closest—their own gangs and sets (and whatever smaller temporary alliances could be made to their benefit).

History aside, this book serves as tribute to Chicago's gang compliment cards: the hand-drawn graphics, the blackletter typefaces, the outlandish names and clever slogans. Intriguingly cryptic to the uninitiated, learning to read the cards gives insight to how they interrelate. For example, a "dipped" (upside-down) or "cracked" (broken in half) symbol or name is a sign of disrespect. Acronyms ending with the letter "K" mean "killer"—so "SDK" for example would be short for "Satan Disciple Killer." One Insane Popes card within these pages is "fixed" with the name Larkin crossed out and "is dead" "G/L's" handwritten beneath, indicating that Popes' leader Larkin was killed by Gaylords. Speaking of which, the Almighty Gaylords and other majority-white gangs frequently utilized racist iconography and language on their cards. Interestingly, Latin Disciples also used swastikas as one of their symbols—some say in homage to their deceased first leader Albert "King Hitler" Hernandez. While the ideologies behind these symbols may have been half-baked coming from the minds of teenagers, racism was a real dynamic in this history (for some more than others) and demonstrations of racial pride (and hate) can't be ignored. On the other hand, a couple cards included here are from neighborhood groups known as party crews (occasionally designated by cocktail glass symbols or P.P. initials). However, this line could be thin at times, with some like Gangster Party People, Party Players, and Stoned Freaks starting out as party crews and transitioning to full-fledged street gangs later on.

More recently, my Pops elaborated on that old business card's origins—telling me his friend had been a junior member of the Royal Capris, a greaser club from the Northwest Side, and that he'd likely get a kick out of my interest. I've since become fascinated with these idiosyncratic cultural relics, and have managed to build a collection of original compliment cards of my own. In the process, I've spoken to retired members from some of these gangs to hear their stories and build my knowledge base (along with reading books and speaking to other historians on this subject). While some of the gangs in these pages are now defunct, others remain active. For various reasons—change of culture, the rise of digital media, etc.—the practice of creating compliment cards had fallen out of favor by the 1990s.

This new edition of the book catalogs a selection of significant or otherwise interesting cards from my collection with a handful of swap outs from the original, and is now ordered geographically (more or less) winding from south to north to reflect both the fundamental link of these organizations with physical locations and their interactions with other gangs nearby (which can be deduced directly from the cards themselves with a close eye to detail). For many the greatest value of these cards will be their role as primary sources that give rare insight into the history of an underground but widespread subculture in Chicago. For others who are (or were) more closely involved the cards record a legacy. Whatever the case, the main intended purpose of this book is to preserve these ephemeral materials to be accessed for years to come as originals disappear to the sands of time.

—Brandon Johnson

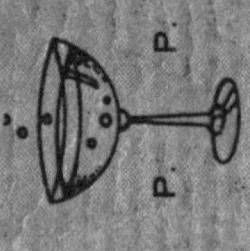

PLAYBOY • PACO • MR. SHY
MR. J • LIL BEAR

Compliments
From the
Spanish Lovers
of Sixty-Third

MEMO • JOSE
ROCKY • WOODSTOCK • PLAYER

Stevan
Sam
Joe
Israel

Roy
Robert
Speedy
Nasty

Lover's

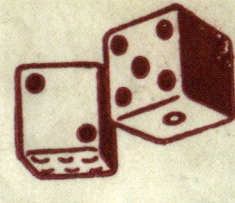

Compliments
of
Thee
Almighty
Party Players
of 48th Street

Pepe   Luckie

Nesto Toker
Marcos Noel
Rankie Rudy
Lando Mario

Player's

Night Crew Association

of

45th St. N Justine
Latin Soul Killers

**Compliments From
Thee Almighty**

Beto Phantom Lil Gangster Mustang
Trigger Comps Lil Man Carbon
  Puppet
  Boner
  Healy
  Styx
  Zepro
  Casper

Wizer
Muff
J.C.
Ram
Oz
Chico
Kayo
Drac

Beto
Shorty

Shadow Ki Ki
Baby "G"

Compliments of

Phantom

From Thee Insane Miniature

Night Crew

Latin Soul Killer

L.S.K.

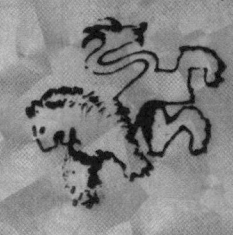

SHY-LAD	OUR COMPLIMENTS	CAPONE
CANO	WE GIVE	LIL DAGO
BIG DAGO	FROM THEE	JOE-ZEP
YOUNG BLOOD	ALMIGHTY	CHINO
RENE		LIPS
NANDO	"𝕮𝖍𝖎-𝕿𝖔𝖜𝖓"	LIL ROOSTER
ELVIS		JOSE
BIG B	𝖂𝖆𝖗 𝕷𝖔𝖗𝖉𝖘	LIL MAN
LOUIE		CANE
LITO CAPONE		S-D-K

mayo
C.K

Compliments
Of Thee
Almighty Gangster
Two ♦ ♦ Six
Nation

P.K
t-bone

malo
K.K

B.K
lucky

Tex   Conu   *Compliments of*   Lil Jap

Thee Blud.
Latin Counts
of
25th & Cal.

K-K
D-K

Lil Tex   Cesar   Lil Babe

Satan Disciples

Baby Brute
Lil Dragon

Compliments Of Thee
Insane 24th Street

Indio

B∴K
Insane To The Brain
Born To Raise Hell
Nation Wide

Lil Mousie
Lil Monk

Joker

Baby Joe
Snake
Chago

KGK

Sucre
Lil Lobo

Mr. Tarzan

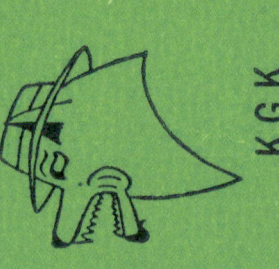

Villa-Lobos
Nation
T S K

Big Cesar
Half-Pint

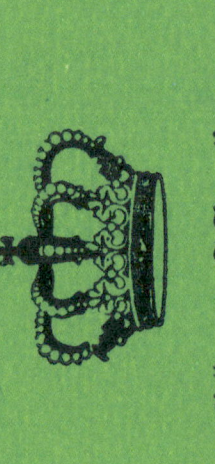

Baby Joker
Tony
Capon

S D K

Tom.
Chico

Bear

Lil-Man

Compliments of
Thee Almighty Miniture
Villa=Lobos
Masters in crime
Killers of slime
And loving thee fine
Young ladies all times

Byrd

Salsa

Lil Romeo	Tony	Mr. Kool	Lil Nick	Lil Guy
Nino		Mr. Cobra	Tunco
	Compliments		Nick	
	of thee Almighty		Mezo	
Kool	King Cobra's			
	of Throop-Cermak		Nino	
Shorty				Lil Guy
Chito				Tunco

Compliments of thee Almighty King Cobra's of Throop-Cermak

Lil Romeo Tony Mr. Kool Lil Nick Lil Guy
Nino Mr. Cobra Tunco
Nick Mezo
Kool Nino
Shorty Chito

Biggie Bat Tako Capone Loco Carlo

Crazy Man   Sun Down   R.J.

Spy Compliments of The Almighty Bro

Zeke   Lil Sal

Bishops

Wolf   Lil Rat

Lil

L.C.B.   Lil Al

Steve Compliments From Thee Original Fly
Damen Party People

Phil   Yogi

Loco   Tony

Malo   Frisky

Manuel   Wino

PARTY PEOPLE
DAMEN & 21st HOYNE

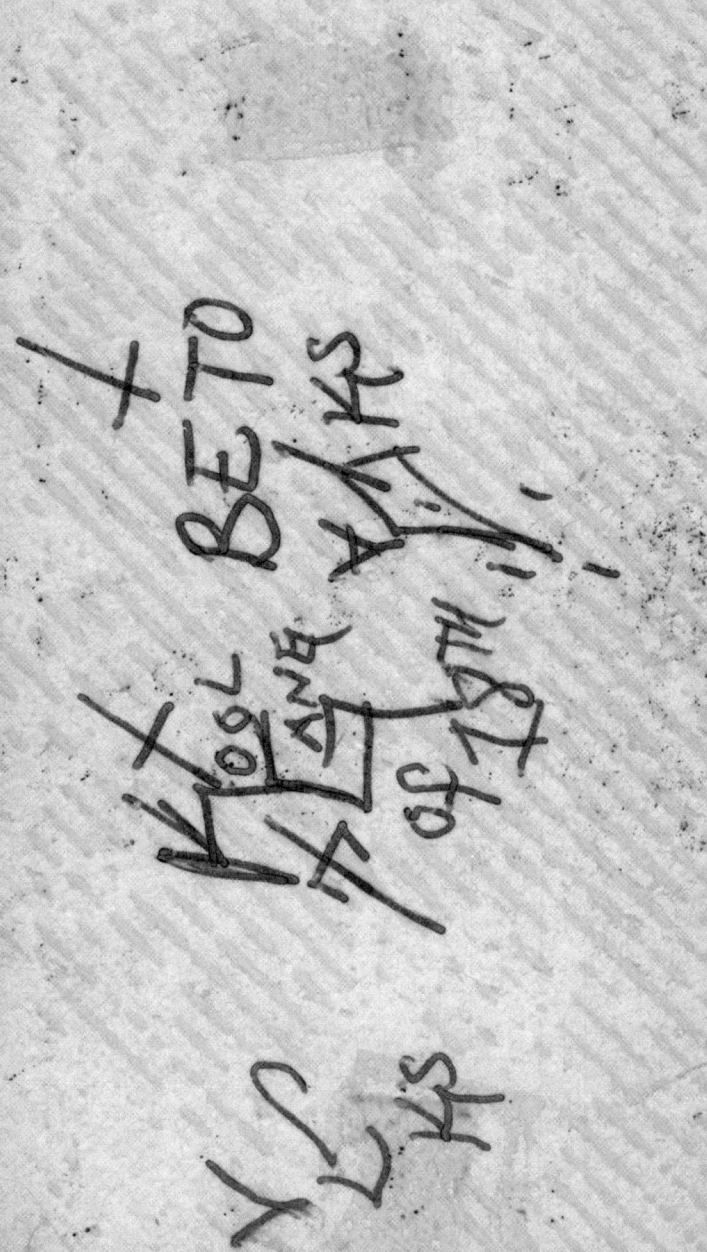

Compliments Of Thee **Party People**

Star Smiley
Launa
Crazy-Lupe
Fighters

Carmen
Lovers

Lil Lupe
Lily
Chayo
Martha
Drinkers

FROM
NANCY

1 TO
KG BETO BETO 79
4.57

Insane Tokers of 19th

I-8H-K

I-6-K

Mr. Bee
Mino
Lee
Lil Bruce
Her
Lil Chico

Lil Mafin
Marcos
Fausto
Lil Gypsy

Buzz

Neil
Compliments of Thee
Almighty Miniature
Kool-Gang
of 18th St.

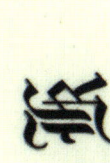

Lil Kapone
Rican
Shorty
Lil Gramps

Thee Almighty Allport Boys

Mando
Weecho
Reno
Abel
Richy
Rafa

Sal

Arthur
Beaver
Manuel
Pablo
Louie
Neto

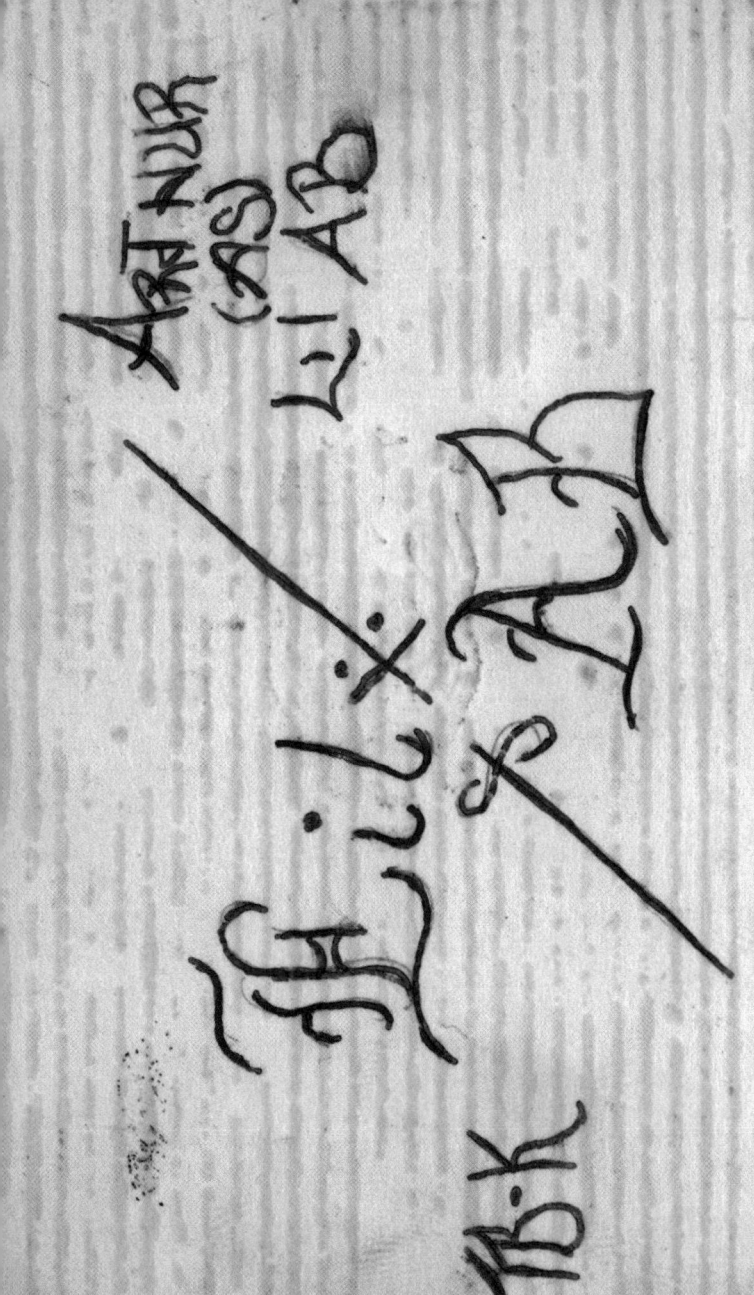

K. C.	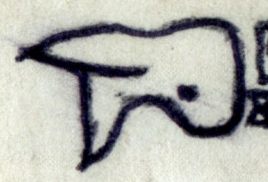	JR.
VITO		

Compliments of

LOS PISTIADORES

MARIO

of

17

— I —

LEFTY	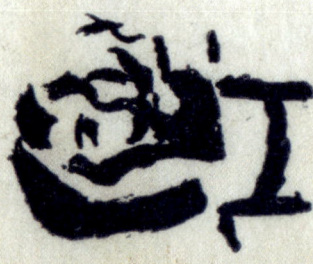	CHRIS
ART		

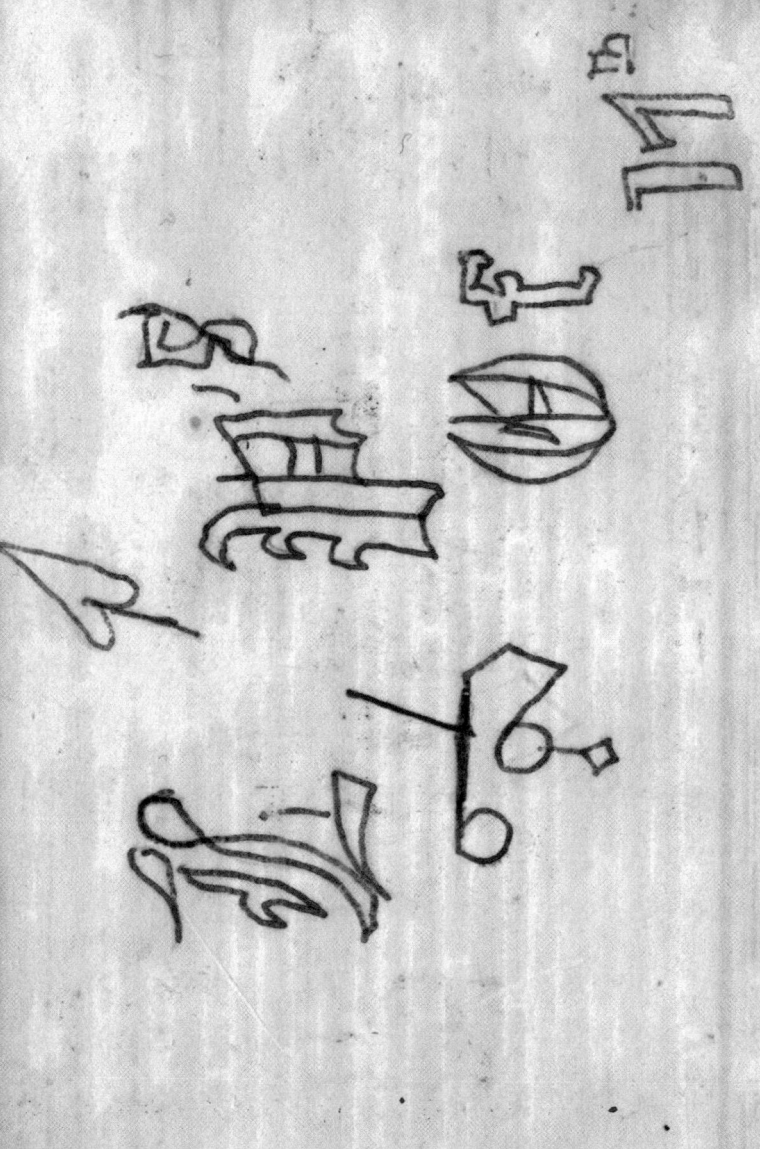

COMPLIMENTS OF

THE ALMIGHTY LITTLE HARRISON GENTS

DEATH BEFORE DISHONOR

OF 26th ST.

〰〰〰〰〰〰〰〰〰〰〰〰

HUSTLERS
-N-
GANGSTERS

HARRISON
-N-
WESTERN

North Side C-Notes

A-RAB
SPADE
BANDIT
GOOBER
CLOWN
BAM BAMM
LIL CAPONE

CAPONE
BUGS
CASPER
PROWLER
SANDOR
CURLEY
SIR LIL JOE

Tiny • Hutch

Thee Almighty Midget **C-Notes**

OHIO & LEAVITT

Burr • Starsky

Andy
Butch

Kent
Brain

Insane   Un Knowns

Simore
Shorty

Cholo
K-Ray

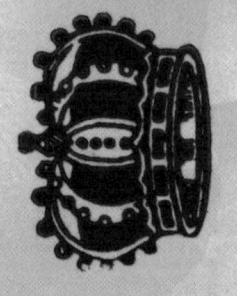

COMPLIMENTS
OF THE
Supreme

"LATIN KINGS"

KING TO THE BONE
NEVER TURN STONE

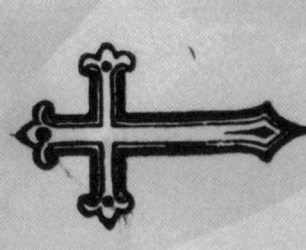

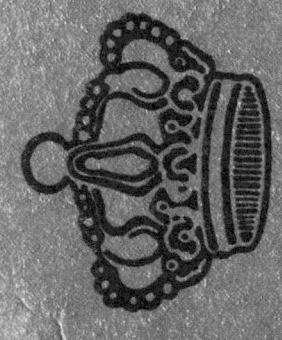

Latin Kings

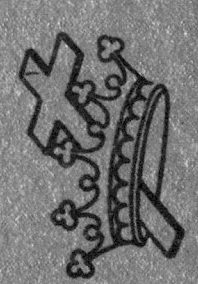

COMPLIMENTS
OF THE
Supreme

KING TO THE BONE
NEVER TURN STONE

K-TOWN LATIN KINGS

CHUCO
PITUFO
LOBITO
LIL MEÑO
LIL MAN
LIL MEX
KYKY

WACHO
LIL TATU
CHICANO
DIABLO
CANO
PONY

SMALL FOLKS

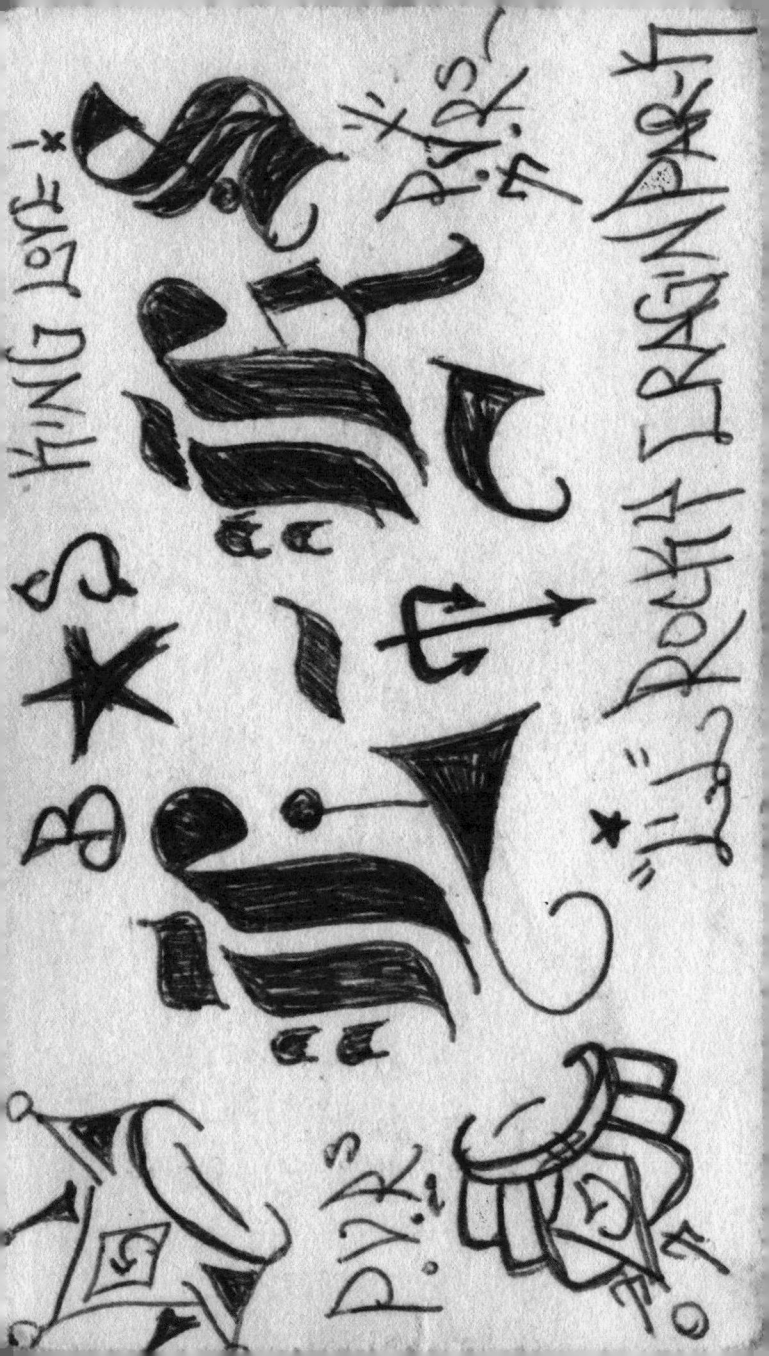

NORTH & KEDVALE · N/K · STONE GREASE

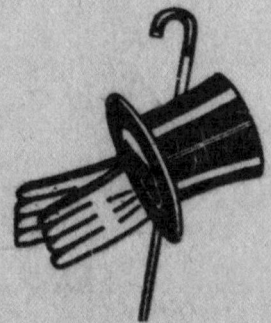

The Almighty
Gaylords

Dago · Chief · Pierre · Lips

Greasers United – Freaks Ain't Shit!

Compliments
of
ELI'S
INSANE
GAYLORDS
CHIEF NORTH
KEDVALE

North & Kedvale

Pyro
Chief

Compliments of the Almighty

Play Boys Ventures Gaylords

Minny
Smiley

Almighty Freaks

Gusto

✝

POTHEAD

B-P-O

Butch   B-L St.

MUGGS

SIR HASH

STONEWALL

✝

F-L

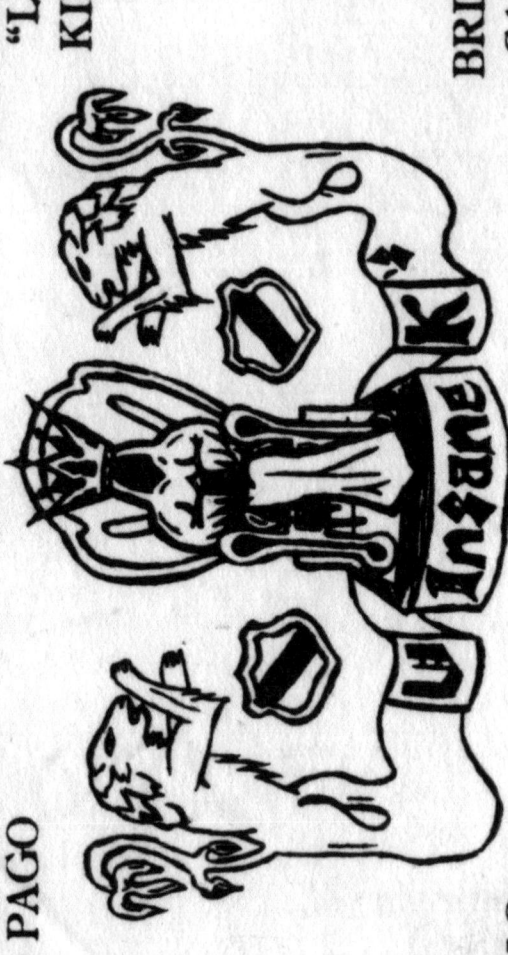

PROUD MEMBERS OF...

HANSON PARK

T.T.
ANZ
AJAX
TIOR
MAT
PAT
KLUTH
BUTCH
BEAR
COMPS. OF...
KID CRAZY
IGK
LDK
CNK

RIDDLER
BLADE
OMEN
ZEUS
LIL JOKER
SCARFACE
CHEWDOG
LIL BEAR
STRAGLER
COMPS. OF...
SIR JOKER
AVH
OAK
LGK

COMPLIMENTS RED ZEPPELIN FLINT SHADOW
OF CAPONE

Almighty Playboys

P.V.P.

KONG
LIVES

DIVERSEY—N—CICERO CRAGIN PAR—K

Compliments of Lil ROCKY

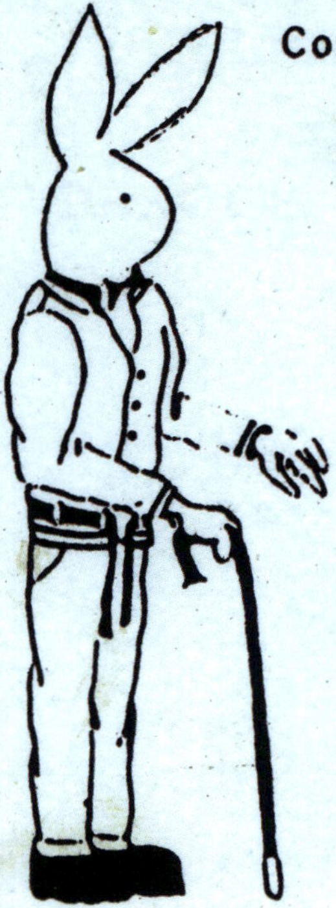

The Almighty
Playhoys

A. P.'s

P. H. K.

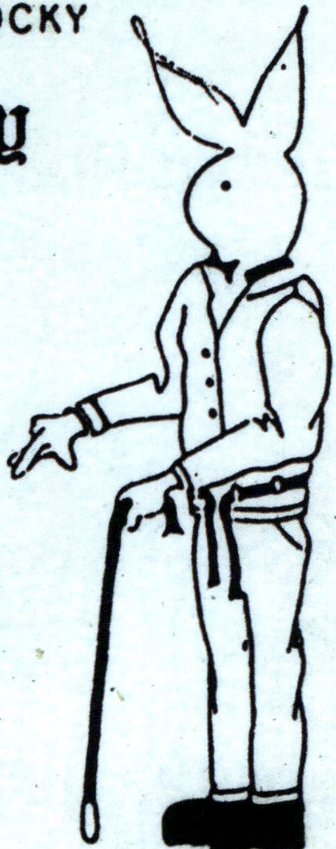

JAY
KNIGHT
RICKY
DOC
Lil NICK

Lil SWAN
GOOFY
Lil MOUSE
SAINT
SPARKY

SQUIRREL · SILVER DRAGON

Thee
Almighty Playboys

LIL SPYDER · REBEL · WINCHESTER

MEMBER: _____

Thee Almighty May Boys

Compliments of Magician

Ron Lives
Lil Bugsy Rebel
Squirrel
Lil Spyder
Sir Hope
Kong Lives

ROYAL CAPRIS

R C's

Legs Diamond

Almighty
Senior
Royal Capris

Belden & Ridgeway

Weasel

Columbo

TACO

GEEK

CHICAGO
SPANISH GANGSTERS

ECUADOR

SOPER FLEA

Compliments of Taco

LAWNDALE
&
FULLERTON

MIGHTY NATION OF LAWNDALE

GAYLORD

MGT. P.W. JRS. SRS.

OUR DYNASTY WILL NEVER PERISH

LAWNDALE
&
ALTGELD

Compliments of the
Almighty Devil

L/A

Lawndale
Gaylords

G=Love

Lawndale & Altgeld

INSANE
SPANISH COBRAS

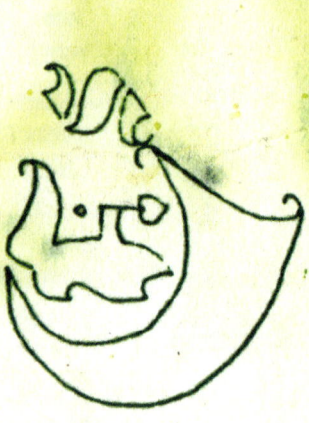

Junior
Loco
Shot Gun

Papo
Demon
Shorty

Central Park
- N -
Schubert

Ridgeway
- N -
Thomas

Baby - C
LIL KK
Bolo

Lil Man
Berreta
Flaco

G - K   L - K - K   I - 2 - K
        Folks Know

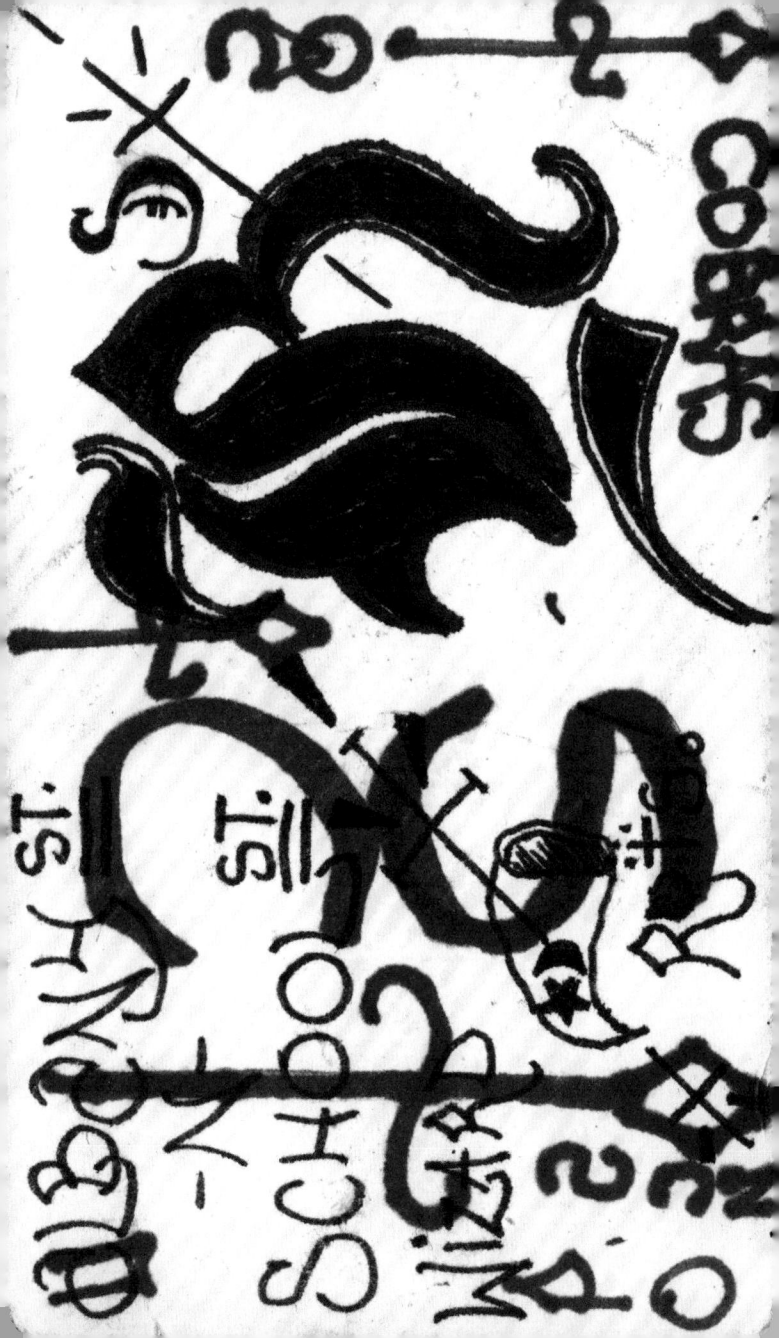

COMPLIMENTS OF THE Jr. Taylor Jousters

TAYLOR & OAKLEY

NORTH SIDE

Jr. Taylor Jousters

FULLERTON & ST. LOUIS

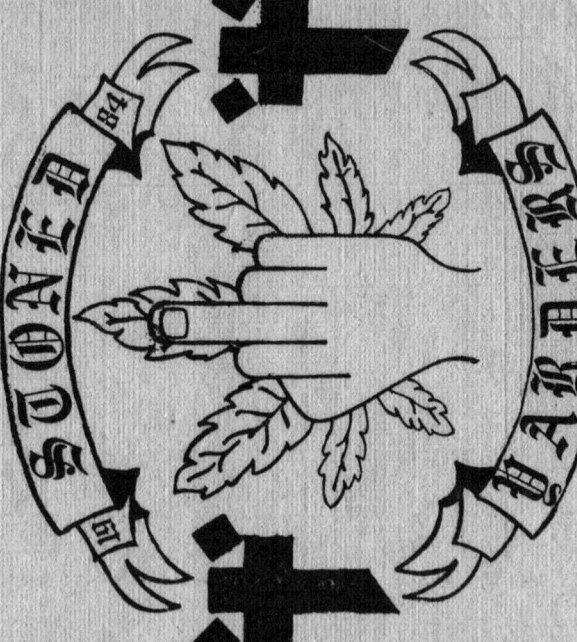

Weed
Muniar
Stoner

Duke
Buzz
Fry

Lord Jim
Magnum
Baby-Blue

Axe
Bre
Champ

Wizard

'Lil' Nate
Iron Man
Buck

The Almighty Logan Square Heads

Klobun

Nighthawk

Jive
Hunchy
Sylvester

Compliment's of thee Almighty
Future Chicago

Shotgun
PRES.

Topcat
VICE-PRES.

Axe

Sinbad

Savage

Chinaman

Flaco Player's Silver

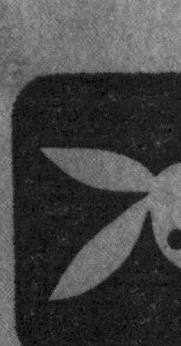

Devoted K-K & G. B. O. Killers

Compliments Of
Palmer Jouster
Partners

Sly=Lilmace
Bullet

Godfather
Hatter

REBEL   COMPLIMENTS   INSANE   GAYLORDS   SLIM
               NORTH + CENTRAL   DON'T!

WHITE

GOD
FORGIVES
   BRANCH
      OF
PALMER ST. GAYLORDS
     LIL
     SLIM
FROG   HILLBILLY   SLICK

G·L·K

COMPLIMENTS OF CAPONE

NORTHWEST SIDE

Maniac Latin Hoods

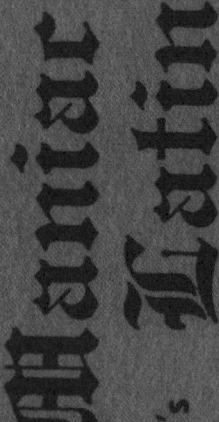

DEVOTED K's K

OF STAVE & FRANCIS
In loving memory of Polaco,
from
Sabu, Huffy, Bird, Rabbit
and
Capone Pres.

O·A's K

PRESIDENT MR. O-A VICE PRESIDENT LIL GAUCHO

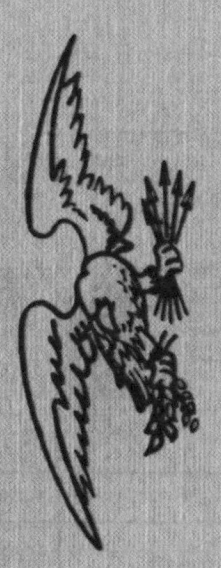

Compliments of
The Almighty Insane Orchestra
Albany Gangsters

future

SMILEY
SHORTY-D
RABBIT
FLACO
K-9
NUCH

X-13 (DEVOTED MLD-KILLERS)
SECTION

WOLFY
SPANKY
KUKU
CASPER
RATT
RED-EYE

DK come get some DK

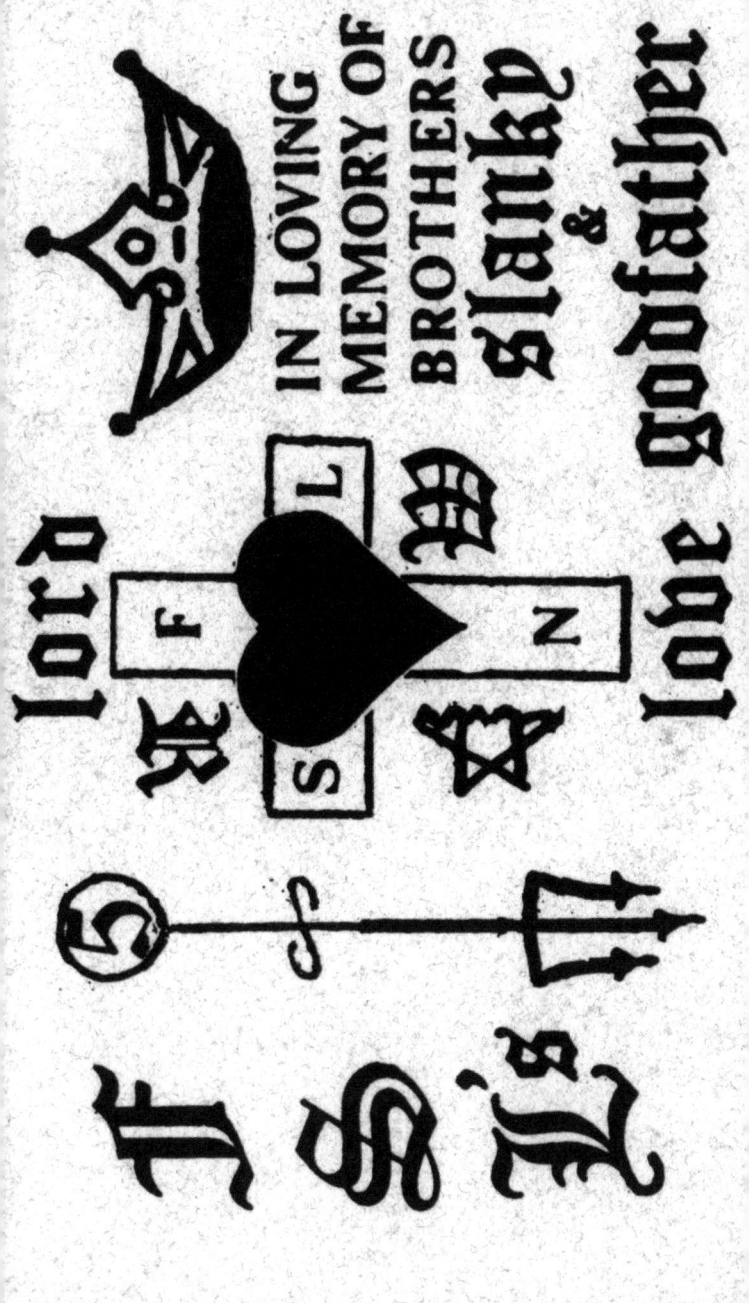

Compliments	Pee-Wee	Damen
of		&
"Sir Sticks"		Clybourn
Munchkin	INSANE	Froggy
Serpico	2	Porky
Lil Flash	DEUCES	Lil Zip
S D B 4 D H C O		

The Almighty Northside Puerto Rican Stones

S☆N

Flintstone
Salami
Loco
Slick

TALL L·E·K S·C·R·K

R.I.P.
Tony P.
Black Tony

Satan
Insane
Pyro
Slick Rick

TALL PEOPLE

R.I.P.
Joey B.
P. R.

ALBANY SCHOOL

SIMON-CITY ROYALS

Ain't no pity in Simon-City

K-K / 2-K
GLK

KOOL-AID	MAD-DOG
OUTLAW	SHORTY
CAPONE	SPANKY
SCORP	GRAN-PA
LIL-LION	BABY-FACE
SARGE	DUBA
LIL-OUTLAW	SCARY-C
LIL-BUZZ	DEVIET

KILBOURN-PARK **SIMON-CITY ROYALS** L.A. AIN'T SHIT.
G L's ARE BITCHES. ASK SPY.

CYCO REMEMBERED ALWAYS.

KOZ PARK
SPY ROYS
K K

WACKY
BIG MONEY
MUGSY
LIL K-K
PUMA
DEVIL
LIL SPOOKY
CASPER
SAINT
CAPONE
SCORP-A-S
PLAYBOY-A-S
STOOGE-A-S
DEVIET-A-S

LIL ACE
LIL LERCH
LIL G L K
SHORTY
SATAN
LIL SIMON
LIL ROCKY
RAT
WEST
MANIAC
LIL RON
DROOPY
OUTLAW-A-S
LIL REBEL
CAPONE-A-S

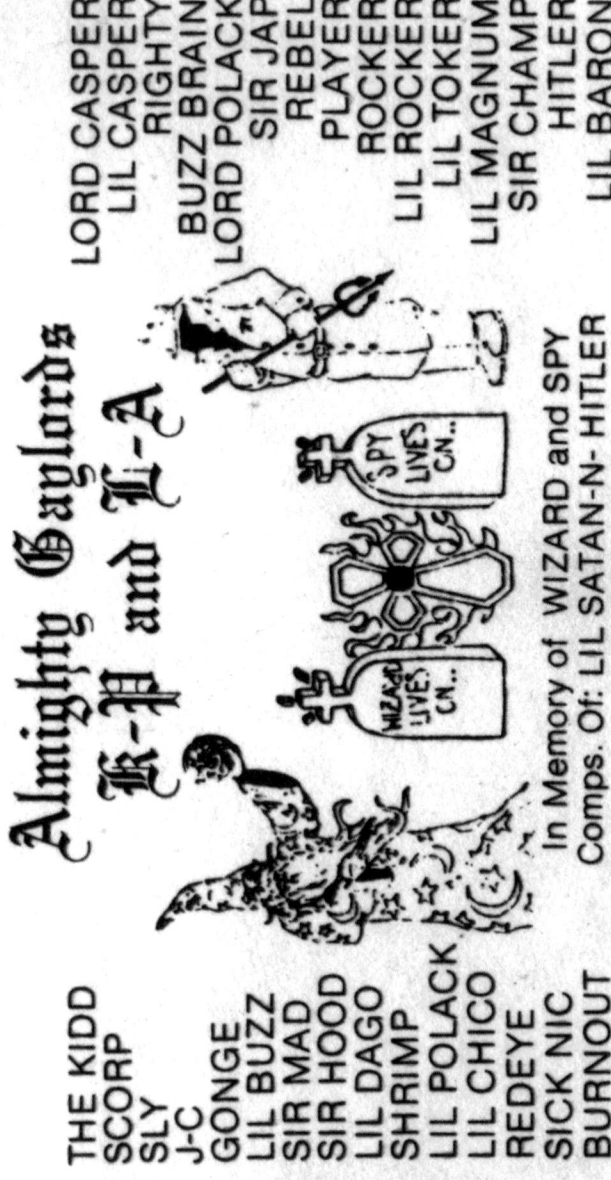

Almighty Gaylords
K-H and L-A

THE KIDD
SCORP
SLY
J-C
GONGE
LIL BUZZ
SIR MAD
SIR HOOD
LIL DAGO
SHRIMP
LIL POLACK
LIL CHICO
REDEYE
SICK NIC
BURNOUT

LORD CASPER
LIL CASPER
RIGHTY
BUZZ BRAIN
LORD POLACK
SIR JAP
REBEL
PLAYER
ROCKER
LIL ROCKER
LIL TOKER
LIL MAGNUM
SIR CHAMP
HITLER
LIL BARON

In Memory of WIZARD and SPY
Comps. Of: LIL SATAN-N-HITLER

Ceacil

Lil Rock

Member of the
Almighty Insane
KILBOURN PARK
Sylords

Wolf

Mugsy

Lil Marco

Lil Ceaser

INDEPENDENCE PARK

BIRDMAN

COMPLIMENTS OF

Insane Pope's

LIL GREASAR

LIL CEASAR

Coyote — Lil Dave

Almighty — Unknown

Pope's

Chicago Wonder — Chicago kid

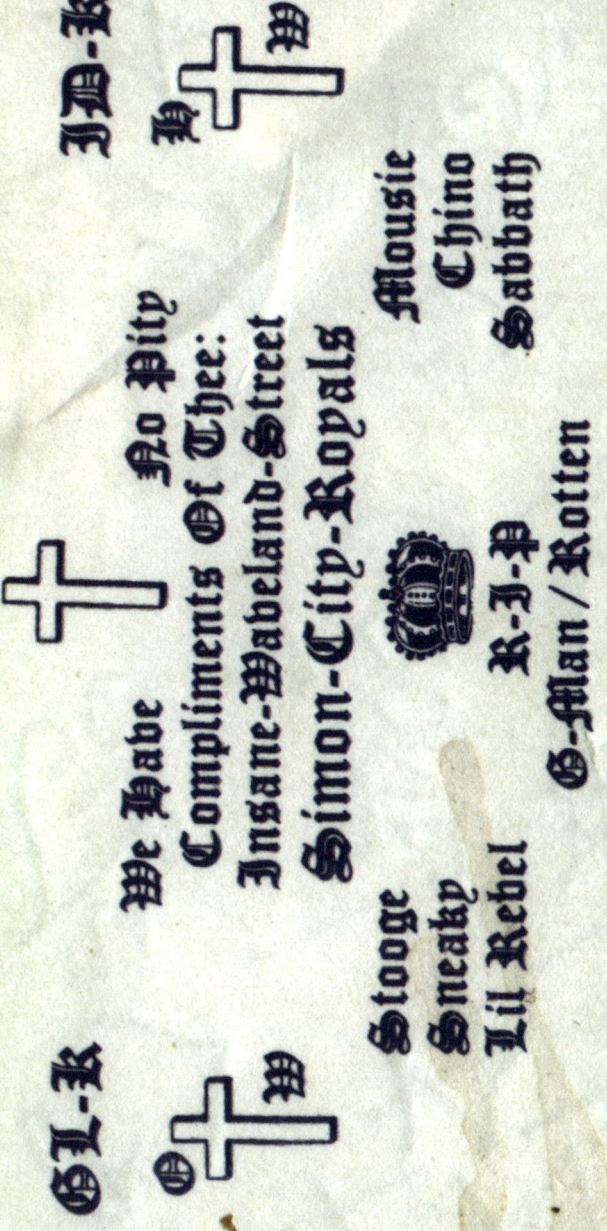

We Have
No Pity
Compliments Of Thee:
Insane-Wabeland-Street
Simon-City-Royals

Stooge
Sneaky
Lil Rebel

Mousie
Chino
Sabbath

R-I-P
G-Man / Rotten

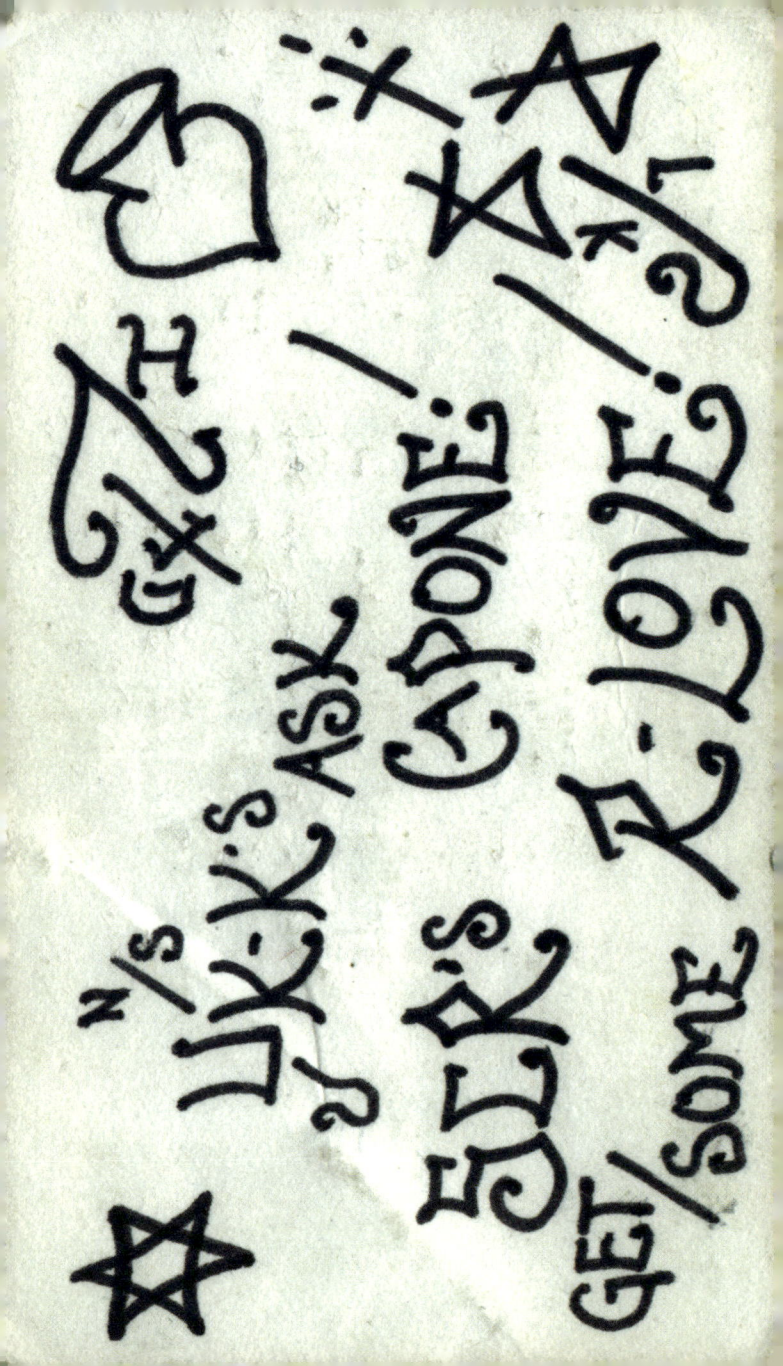

STONED FREAKS

SWORN TO FUN LOYAL TO NONE

- KOOKIE
- RIDGERUNNER
- CHUCKIE
- CHICO
- SPACECAT
- IRONMAN
- BONEHEAD
- MOUSE
- MIDNIGHT RAMBLER

Compliments of: Bodean

Thee Almighty & Insane

UNITED FREAKS
L-C

Hawkeye
Pipeman
Frymind
Ringo

Buzz
Bandit
Lil Bruiser
Shotgun

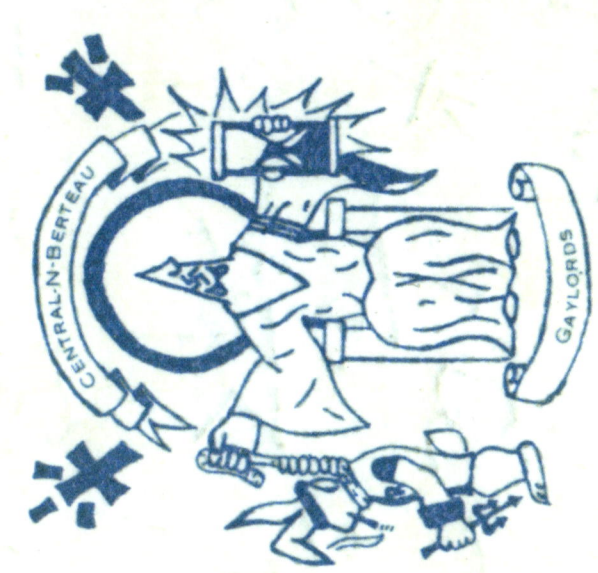

Lord Flash
Midget
Loner
Whitey
Lil Runner
Sir Zepp
Scorpio
Nomad
Spike
Lord Dio

Lil Spanky
Mr. Who
Jester
Lil J-C-W
Lil Flopd
Lil Zepp
Magic
Too Tall
Lil Gob
Mr. Fudd

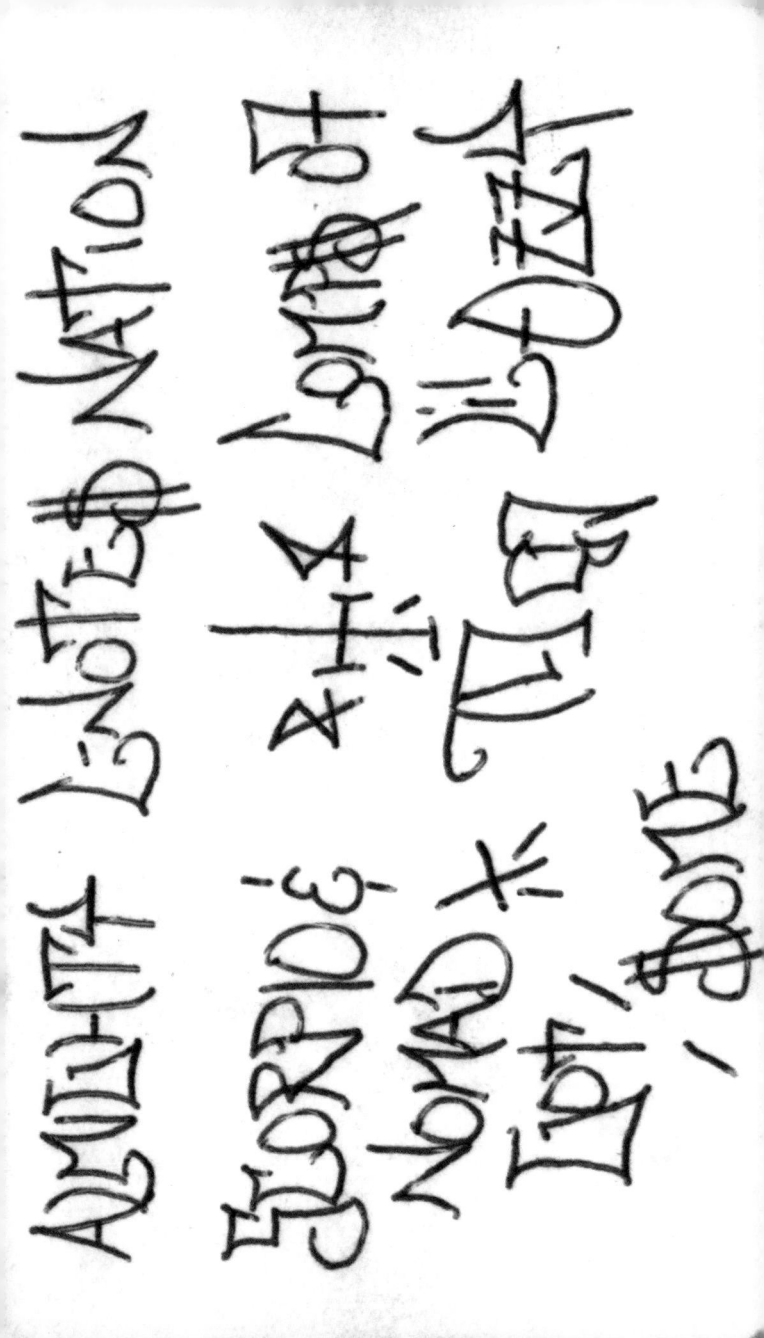

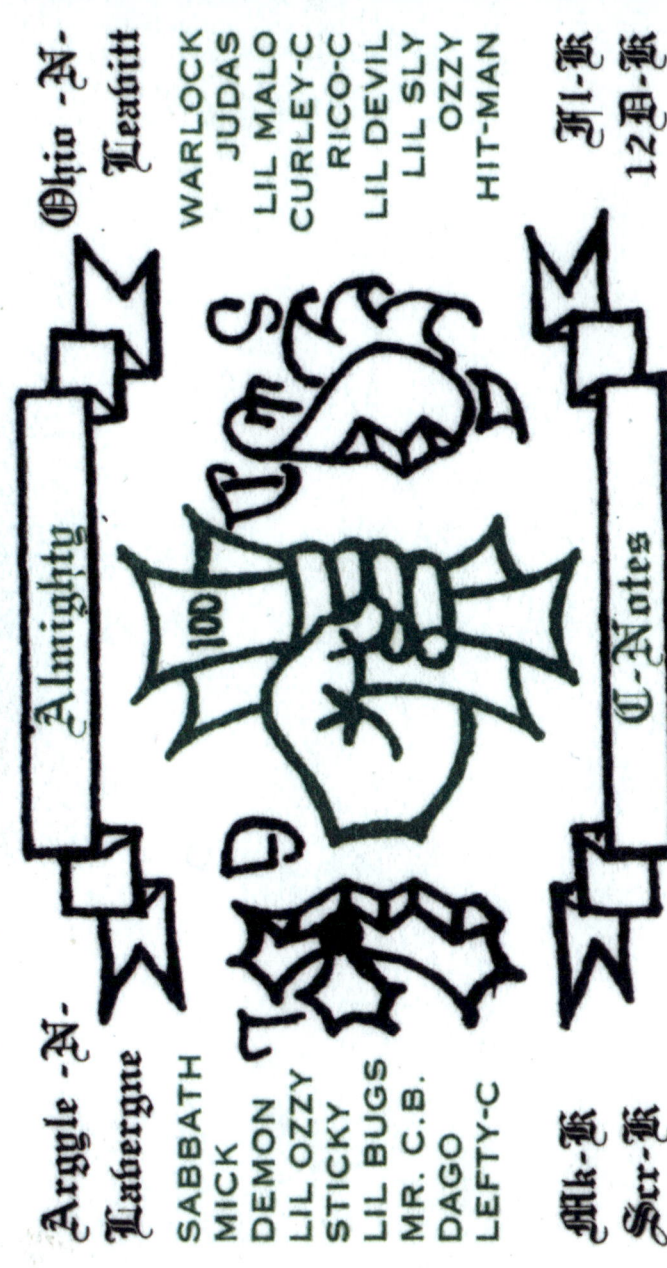

C-Notes Gangsters

L A

"Lunatic"
"Bud Head"

Freaks World....
You just live in it!

"Mr. YAK"
"Thief"

Black and Red....
till Folks are Dead!

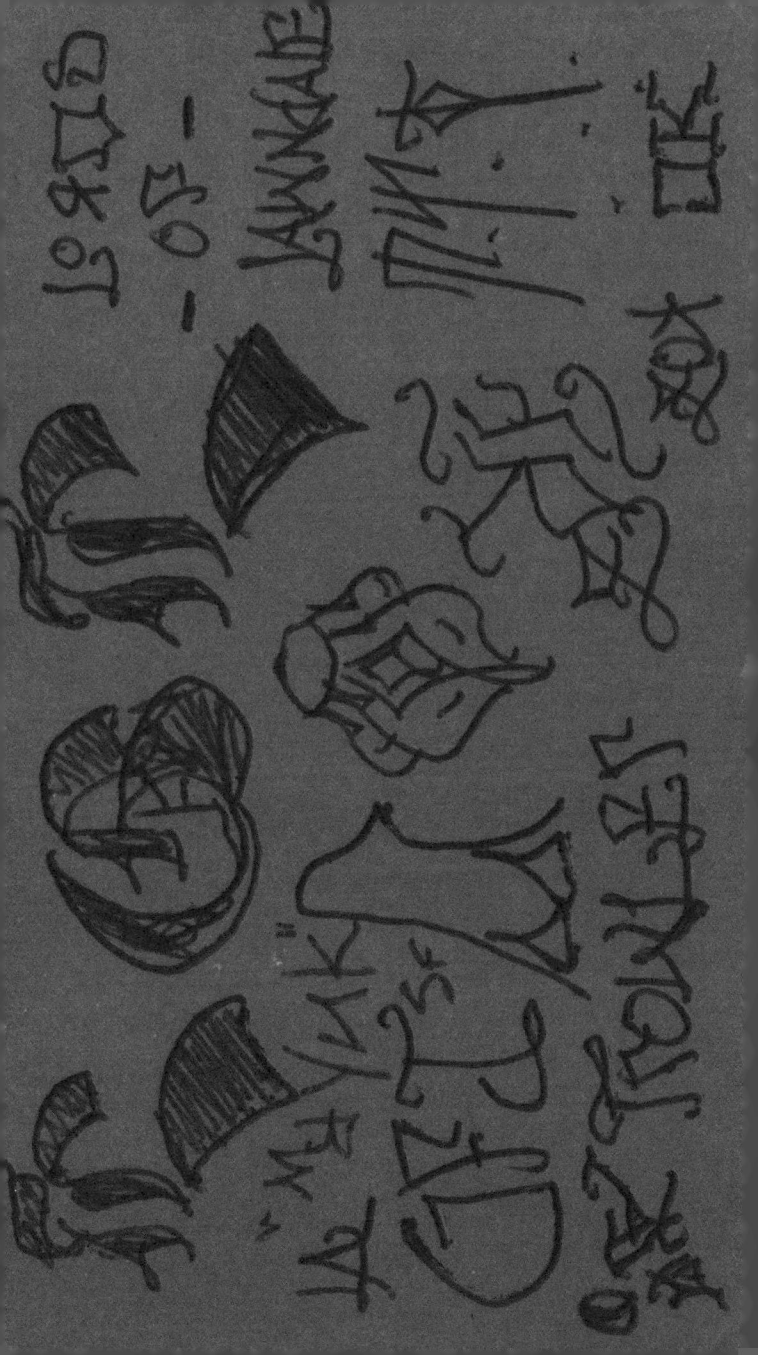

COMPLIMENTS OF:

MONK

'LIL' BOB

The Almighty Popes
North Mayfair

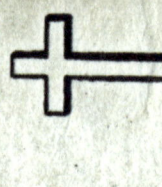

BIGFOOT	BULLDOG	'LIL' HOOD
BABYFACE	SLAUGHTER	ROCKY
MUGSY	SLIM	TERMITE
PYRO	WINGS	FREIGHT

Red

Farmer

Compliments of Fro

Thee

Monticello & Wilson

Freaks

A FRIEND WITH WEED
IS A FRIEND INDEED

Lucky

Loebs

O.M.

F-C

Campbell-Hunt

Simon-City-Royals

Lil Satan - Jungle Jim
Sneaky - Lil Joker

Lil Capone
The Professor
Sandman
Sultan
Gilligan
Paz
Tyrant

Lil Dagger
Weasel
Beast
Pyro
Pest
Casper
Lil Rebel